Blue Hallelujahs

Blue Hallelujahs

Cynthia Manick

Black Lawrence Press

 Black Lawrence Press

www.blacklawrence.com

Executive Editor: Diane Goettel
Book and cover design: Amy Freels
Cover art: "To Trust In" by Ify Chiejina

Copyright © 2016 Cynthia Manick
ISBN: 978-1-62557-135-9

All rights reserved. Except for brief quotations in critical articles or reviews, no part of this book may be reproduced in any manner without prior written permission from the publisher: editors@blacklawrencepress.com

Published 2016 by Black Lawrence Press.

Contents

What I Know About Blues	1
I Feel This Knowing Rising	
Pulling Threads	5
The Shop Washington Built	7
Bop: Big Sister Dreams	9
Inside the Rolling Walls: A Fairytale	10
Ethel September	12
The Sun Don't Know	13
What Lies Beneath	15
Things I Carry Into the World	16
Mind the Gap	17
Spooling Back the Threads	19
A Body Full of Verbs	
2 am	23
A Dark Blush	24
The Husband in Contrast	25
Let Me Dance While I Dream	26
Recipe for Consummation	27
Tapping at Mama's Knees	28
Venue Change	30
The Hip Collective	31
Revolution Staccato in B	32

So Many Colors All Over
Middle Passage — 35
Glory — 36
The First Paradise — 38
To Speak About What Isn't Spoken — 39
King of the Natural World — 41
I Saw You on the Delta Queen — 42
Hunger — 43
What We Push Against — 44
The Reaper in Me — 45

The Secret of Living in This Body
Imperfection Begins Early — 49
Letter to 1991 — 50
The Human Condition — 51
The Future of Skin — 52
House of Magic Rocks — 54
Dear Black Dress — 55
Pitkin Avenue and Stone — 57
How a Poet Carries Weight — 59

Blue Hallelujahs
I See a Dirt Road Inside Myself — 63
Scrape the Brown Bottom — 64
When I Think of My Father — 66
Dark Fruit — 68
Passing — 70
The Museum — 71
Blue Hallelujahs from the Hand — 73

Acknowledgments — 75

What I Know About Blues

I know butterflies can taste
with their feet.
Blackberry vinegar or apple water
can break a fever.

I know the sharp length
of my mother's tongue
*use every part of the fruit
and stem* she'd say, *don't leave
anything behind.*

I know the skin of mackerel
is softer than an eyelid.
I know salt—the way it sifts
through tips, piling
on a wife's lap like gold.

Can you hear how I hold
a breath inside—
use my body to say
*I can be your Clementine
I can be your sweet baby.*

Yes,
I know how to name things.
I've been called little lady,
pickaninny, gel, mamacita, the black one,
the big one, the dark one, woman—
each name makes a map of me.

I Feel This Knowing Rising

Pulling Threads

My mother's mother is a doll
not yet painted, too light to be brown
too dark to be white,
a beige-red heft not in the rainbow.
*You need to stick that girl
in the fire*, people would say.
All the townies wondered why
she married Grandpa Willie, that slick
umbered pearl who pulled bushels
of oysters from the sea.

Did he court her, twirl her fine
brown strands in hand,
bring jars of bloodroot for porches
tin basins of crab and coconuts
soap carvings of mallards and snails,
or did they crawl into faraway sounds
as he laid her down and baked
her skin in the sun?

Yesterday I found a photograph
in the upstairs dresser:
her white whalebone corset
pink gloves that lace at the elbow
his pomade hair slicked to the right
the juke-joint slide
gold-plated incantations of *baby baby*
and the bark of bodies bursting like plums.

It takes time now to see past their layers—
his Saturday nets, a quarter full
her rosary of apple seeds

their hands do that slow shaky thing
but I can almost see veins
like water weeds climbing up the throat,
trying to find the heat
and stirring, the body remembers.

The Shop Washington Built

Wild Willie Washington
        branded his two-toned laugh
on corn and rye
        from warm copper pots.

He owned *The Shop* with three daughters,
        a crowded hall of bootleg
crab and boiled turtle eggs.
        Some say honeycomb cells

from bees who spoke Greek.
        At sundown he'd wipe the bar,
hands flaps of hard ringed skin
        and told small tales of lurid affairs

with Lena Horne and Ms. Ross.
        Lessons on the proper way
to eat mushrooms, wear dragon
        hide as a belt, or spell out

the word Mississippi *m-i-*
        crooked letter-crooked letter-
Or his art of playing pool,
        the sound of ball to cue

should be a low clicking
        small round wings, cascading
magpies light as walnut shells.
        When you played

he crunched on boisterous
        chips, tapped his black booted
feet to a tune and stared you
        down until you flinched.

During the summers you hear
        his laughter ringing between
broken beams and marsh reeds
        the size of two tall ships.

Bop: Big Sister Dreams

I'm a hardwearing Dixie peach in a one-room
shop full of hops looking for great migrations.
There's a turning in my belly, when pings
of the till rings only twice daily—Bud, cola,
or wooden spoons. A dollar bill stretches wide
while hunger grows another layer of skin.

We all wander and juggle in the lights
until every floor is soaked through

The paper plant in North Santee is callin,
the assembly line takes root, a blind room
pan-fried like many others. I've always wanted
to be mistress of Fate or Mount Olympus,
a deity dressed in Woolworth's best chiffon
or smooth pink lace. To have my own till
where Dap Daddies and big-bellied men
can swig and swing like Jesus lives here.

We all wander and juggle in the lights
until every floor is soaked through

When they unfold my limbs and cut me open—
a cow-heavy old woman in a gliding chair,
they'll find an open mouth, manmade twine,
and a small whiskey cask turned down—
where I keep topaz peaches and a restless
pulse banked low like a secret.

We all wander and juggle in the lights
until every floor is soaked through

Inside the Rolling Walls: A Fairytale

On a good day *The Shop* sold bootleg
gin, fresh pulled frog legs, and used fedoras.
When the middle daughter tended the bar,
hands cut the best meat for po' boys.

Her gin sweeter than candy yams,
she could cut a rug with every papa
and uncle in the place. Her only want—
glitter from up north

bright lights of tall buildings
to cast a shadow her sisters could see.
But one day she met a boy
who made her liver quiver. He was tall

like her daddy—had a left side
swagger full of nectarines and apple
vinegar. His runner legs and Paul Chambers
bass promised slick cocoa butter;

their fingers white from the steam of it.
At night they kissed 'til lips bruised and
made their own grease. All was alive
in hands and caked feet. Light culled

in her belly. Something banked inside—
an incense of follicles to flesh. The news
slipped over his head like water. Her hip-
grinding pelvis became one swollen bowl.

Bop: Big Sister Dreams

I'm a hardwearing Dixie peach in a one-room
shop full of hops looking for great migrations.
There's a turning in my belly, when pings
of the till rings only twice daily—Bud, cola,
or wooden spoons. A dollar bill stretches wide
while hunger grows another layer of skin.

We all wander and juggle in the lights
until every floor is soaked through

The paper plant in North Santee is callin,
the assembly line takes root, a blind room
pan-fried like many others. I've always wanted
to be mistress of Fate or Mount Olympus,
a deity dressed in Woolworth's best chiffon
or smooth pink lace. To have my own till
where Dap Daddies and big-bellied men
can swig and swing like Jesus lives here.

We all wander and juggle in the lights
until every floor is soaked through

When they unfold my limbs and cut me open—
a cow-heavy old woman in a gliding chair,
they'll find an open mouth, manmade twine,
and a small whiskey cask turned down—
where I keep topaz peaches and a restless
pulse banked low like a secret.

We all wander and juggle in the lights
until every floor is soaked through

Inside the Rolling Walls: A Fairytale

On a good day *The Shop* sold bootleg
gin, fresh pulled frog legs, and used fedoras.
When the middle daughter tended the bar,
hands cut the best meat for po' boys.

Her gin sweeter than candy yams,
she could cut a rug with every papa
and uncle in the place. Her only want—
glitter from up north

bright lights of tall buildings
to cast a shadow her sisters could see.
But one day she met a boy
who made her liver quiver. He was tall

like her daddy—had a left side
swagger full of nectarines and apple
vinegar. His runner legs and Paul Chambers
bass promised slick cocoa butter;

their fingers white from the steam of it.
At night they kissed 'til lips bruised and
made their own grease. All was alive
in hands and caked feet. Light culled

in her belly. Something banked inside—
an incense of follicles to flesh. The news
slipped over his head like water. Her hip-
grinding pelvis became one swollen bowl.

The boy turned man—placed his horn
in a cage, a shimmer he tries to sever.
Rented a house by the river, a home
to blossom inside. The girl—now a wife

mother irons clothes for him and coins;
her fingers red from the steam of it.
Days are long in the truck bed, his back
a two-ton blade of gin made for lifting.

Their house turned into an island of *jesus
marysavesouls* where she all wanted was maiden
blood and name. To shake loose the afterbirth,
scorched black beans, stones of the words

in-sickness-in-health. Now when he lurches
into her covered in some other woman's
tropic perfume, it's bare legs against hands
full of gravel. Vows break like husks.

Ethel September

Your rocking chair sways by itself now,
a phantom southern belle of floral cotton

the snapping of peas nipping at tips. In your
youth, twirling in taffeta and silk, a pastel fan,

a curve of lip, you're a debutante. Feet bare
of cloth, you run through fields, ants on ankles—

belly moving to the sound of bullfrogs. Holding
your hand and a strand of poppies, your brother

leads you to a tree where peaches fly. And there
you sit, stuffing pits of cherries into the side

of your cheeks and nose. Have you seen Mr. Nat?
They placed him in a wicker chair, brown toes

cocked up towards the Carolinas. The cancer flies
gathered in his pockets, death followed and settled.

Is he there yet? Now you are on the porch. That house
of white shutters and long-necked bottles of coke.

My father lies on your lap, head lolled to crickets, and
you begin to sing, *"mah honey, mah honey, mah honey."*

The Sun Don't Know

the way lies can curl—
      a comma
      in your pocket
but it don't change
      the skin you're in

at the brink of crossing
make sure your slip
      isn't showing
somebody's mama is watching

don't be afraid to drink
whiskey or sweet tea
      dark enough
      to embalm a man

legs stretching over mine—
      hello honey dipper

sometimes pain is—
sand dollar smooth
a flooded mouth
      devoured rinds
           brown rivers
      beneath cotton

listen to what is gone
      our bones
      numbered
      cattle culled

grandmother says *they fear*
        our womb   the reckoning
       hive of dark
berries and stems

true things blaze red
like an unwalled
       storm
        in your head

What Lies Beneath

Today I am elbow deep
in some animal's belly

pulling out the heart and stomach
for my mother's table.

Brown rubber soles blood slicked,
the swing of twin blades

cuts a whole village worth of pelts,
coon, carved bones for ladies

jewelry and coats. These hands
can ground down rock and gold

call a man *sweet dusty*, mold
knots of spit and hair like clay

until a baby's head is perfectly round.
These hands are good for killing—

I feel this knowing rise
like different names for fire.

Every bone has a ghost—
the smallest, a stirrup in the ear

whispers *walk carefully there, you
know you come from a dark tribe.*

Things I Carry Into the World

when I was small
I thought my body held
all the elements

my left instep knew
how to make snow
drop like pendulums

rain shaped like spoons
the volume of Niagara Falls
a heat so heavy

it's in our blood you know
the power to grow
fibroids ossified fruit

to hold lightning inside
grow daughters among
shifting currents

like thunderclouds
I don't stray far from earth-
ly things

I still whet my teeth
on branches in the yard
wonder how planets are made

What Lies Beneath

Today I am elbow deep
in some animal's belly

pulling out the heart and stomach
for my mother's table.

Brown rubber soles blood slicked,
the swing of twin blades

cuts a whole village worth of pelts,
coon, carved bones for ladies

jewelry and coats. These hands
can ground down rock and gold

call a man *sweet dusty*, mold
knots of spit and hair like clay

until a baby's head is perfectly round.
These hands are good for killing—

I feel this knowing rise
like different names for fire.

Every bone has a ghost—
the smallest, a stirrup in the ear

whispers *walk carefully there, you
know you come from a dark tribe.*

Things I Carry Into the World

when I was small
I thought my body held
all the elements

my left instep knew
how to make snow
drop like pendulums

rain shaped like spoons
the volume of Niagara Falls
a heat so heavy

it's in our blood you know
the power to grow
fibroids ossified fruit

to hold lightning inside
grow daughters among
shifting currents

like thunderclouds
I don't stray far from earth-
ly things

I still whet my teeth
on branches in the yard
wonder how planets are made

Mind the Gap

Little E wants a smile like mine,
teeth with a gap so wide
a corn husk and tugboat
could pull through.
Or a submarine, lost sounds
and grunts. Tiny light bulbs
if you're careful or a string
of Christmas lights looped
through like garland.

Does she know how the world
works? How some of us
are born without 40 acres
and the weight of a mule
on their chest. Like my mother
and Monday mornings—
boarding the F train and two buses
with two children, her own negro
caravan. A sonata full of low-watt
clinics and hurling vowels
like swords. How I often waited
in those long-ass lines
and imagined myself a boy,
a whirlwind digging in the muck
where only muscles and gold matter.

My tongue tries to reason with her
ring against her want—cause
we don't choose what haunts us.
When I was young I craved closed

spaces, bright veneers, the smile
of Rudy Huxtable or on bad days
Shirley Temple. No one notices
a mouth when Bojangles is dancing.

Spooling Back the Threads

I'm eighteen when I travel
to Cairo, and leave behind
my father's name

ancient routines
peanut shells on porches
my mother's wooden spoon.

Flu-bitten brows where I'm
a swashbuckling buccaneer
and escapades take root.

I parry my sword. A scarred
thermometer forms
a snug bed in my tongue.

And now I'm eleven
conjuring labored horses
thieves and magical men.

We travel through countrysides
battling hordes, rescuing
troves of bright jewels.

Now I'm seven
surrounded by leaves
scattering like scarabs.

In a small cave where
eggs are made, larvae hatches
I become entomologist.

I use my tools:
> brother's glasses
> plastic pink shovel
> number 2 crayon—red

Now I am four years old
splashing hands through
restless surface of lakes—

not rivers
wondering why I was born
without gills.

A Body Full of Verbs

2 am

I make more animal
        sounds than human

trying to find
those parts of my shadow

that were song
        bobby pins
        a heart-
beat heard ten
        steps behind

Who knew 2 am words
        had texture

of small chili pods
dark as new bruises

Who knew 2 am words
        had loud savagery

fur in the corners
skin overtaken
rind easily sliced

I curve grief
        in my fist
like a dead wolf
        cub

holding close the hour
it stopped
thrashing

A Dark Blush

our music used to
make beds
in tongues

elbow patch
glory knees
seeping savannas

amorous phantoms
bourbon kisses
murmurings of rain

bright white
socks in bed
a pregnant air

you and sepia girls
under almond trees

pristine sheets
empty spaces
a hollowed concave

where music stops
singing
our waltz

The Husband in Contrast

    Slack-jawed veins are made
stiff from cold rooftops in December.

    The body's mercury pools like a bucket
of rooster feet I chopped as a kid.

    My palms are set rooms for electric
saws, hammers, construction bags packed

    like a throat with grain. Cement slow-
cooks behind the dip of my knuckles.

    Is this what the heart eats? If you jostle
my bones, my fingers and toes will throw

    silver-plated ash. The horn of the 10:32
train disrupts my dreams of girls with pecan-

    tans, their skin tricked in pollen under
orange trees, or the dark gingerbread of jazz

    I used to play in the mornings. At home
you're in the kitchen among sweets and pearl-

    shaped cloves, the burnt aroma of Uncle
Ben's rice and sausage. Our seed with its

    rattle speaks in tongues. Etta James is
on the radio and you're mouthing the words

    "You look so sweet and so doggone fine."

Let Me Dance While I Dream

On listening to KoKo Taylor

On the first inhale
start your ritual—
unravel patient rows of braids
remove tight rings or bracelets,
      cause this song wants a body
      full of verbs, each sound
      a gust in the joints.

As one beat balls the jack
read the noise in your head—
shy variations to verse
the double-dose refrain
bridge notes longer than a spine.
KoKo's white-toothed love
coils on repeat,
      forms a bed in your tongue
      and thighs like a tangerine
      rind just bitten.

At the edge, watch it moss
over. Resist the urge to
call your mama or your man.
It's the music that owns you.
Tattoo *Please* and *I Believe*
on your arms and forehead—
      prostrate on a cooling board
      while your bra strap leaks
      cinnamon on the floor.

Recipe for Consummation

Your seasoned skin—
>one quart Egyptian
>the shade of balsa honey,
>one part Cubano
>with a dash of cayenne pepper,
>and one half buttered South—

is a scratch 'n sniff insert
more savory than Old Spice
>or Sara Lee;

and I claw it nightly
like oranges or sand
to whispered chants
>of *sweet meat sweet meat*

and bareback tongues
>in our bedroom,

until shuck sheds
>like a coiled rope
>of dark stars.

I drink it down
pelvic-deep,
>so that my body
>remembers
>the brown bounty

of your herbs and spine
in the morning.

Tapping at Mama's Knees

On Saturdays we slept in whole-tone scales
mama side-slipping in bed to the cool
wash of sheets and Charlie Parker.
She dubbed it sick day. Our symptoms:
hemorrhaging soul patrol
bicoastal funk-edermis
and perforated jazz-endectomy.
We'd lay like a pair of black lizards
or one stuffed cottonmouth.
Belly cluster pillows
with tales of a Jackson Pullman porter
or river boat gambler
or logger from Cameroon she met in '52,
the tale—it always changes.
They all tickled toes like Dizzy's
trumpet carved in gold,
made a girl scream silver amen's
like praise all over the body.
She left behind a handful of land-
locked country boys
and saltwater negroes.
One gave her a ring and a necklace
of coins, cobalt nickel, or amethyst,
the tale—it always changes.
But he couldn't stop the clinging
of saxophones and smoke
that sucked mama straight to Harlem,
curled in the hems of silk slips
and heels of toe-peeped shoes.
While a body craves light
mama wanted the dark arms of trumpeters,
watching the veins pull notes together

was like an island being born.
Even now on Saturdays when low-strings
are bent double, she calls and asks
Why aren't you married? and
What's your favorite horn?

Venue Change

People like dulcet tones
      of country ballads and men,

 the waxy smell of pop
      songs and glam but this place

creates unstable storms
      in my skin, while bone

and mind flash to 3 am jams
      with Monk and Coltrane.

Bass and alto sounds of *ain't you my baby*
      where even the creamed Key

 lime pie tastes like mystery,
      and gin hits my throat like out-

lawed melodies or mouths
      on running water. Real song

 seeps into day, salts the night.
      At my dive we get our jive

 boost inhaling pure sax while whalers
      fling sugar and hops

over shoulders, until the floor trembles
      and every hip moves silent as bells.

The Hip Collective

The hip is critically acclaimed. Made primarily of two mounds: tumbled and heavy. (too much for the pumice stone) You can find them hidden beneath ponchos, on posters, or on T.V. Pam Grier was one bad motha__. Dark skinned plums plump nicely like the shadow Bessie used to wear. Bands played like a secret to see the girls shimmie shimmie. Ella's silhouette stopped crowds:

> core the pit of a peach
> *taste the nimble*
> place the weight
> *in the hand*
> search the dark spot
> *the jived jimmy*
> that's where the heat lies

The curve likes to keep the heart clenchin. Blow apart, spectrum, the physics of the walk. Dance until the mind feels clean. Tease the brown. Refuse to be tamed by some low down tickle, back door man, or honey dripper. Hips don't fight:

> water's rhythm
> bias cut skirts
> too tight to cinch in
> pink porcelain dolls
> blonde Barbie's on nitrates
> the rose rose rose

It wants to go to France and fight the Euro over there. 'Cause black matter holds the universe together. Grandma always said, "in the ancestral house lies our core." People fear the heat and stirring of homegrown Black silhouettes.

Revolution Staccato in B

One thousand saxophones infiltrate the city,
    two by two and each with a pulse of its own.

Some have bodies big as elephant ears
    and heavy-lipped missiles shoot from their pitch.

Others take the long way down.
    Sopranos drop octaves along the banks,

making concave grooves settle into the click
    of thigh bones and cypress knees.

They leave behind G scales in the grass,
    mounds full of girls mouthing *yes yes*.

The altos want to turn New Orleans red
    play *Summertime* in the streets,

have it gulp into bellies like ribs swathed
    in barbeque, liberate bodies from inside out.

They all want night to end full, to riff reeds
    on every corner, every concert hall,

have it settle like gold dust from clit to clavicle.
    Watch them turn the city into a panama of sound,

a house of blues, until it swells like an open mouth
    and babies are scatting in their sleep.

So Many Colors All Over

Middle Passage

for the ancestors of little black girls

All I want is rain
all I want is rain and air and sleep and air
and water

all I want is water
water in my mouth like a rough bruise
water catching on my eyelids
like the purest waterfall
all I want is a waterfall

to fall to pieces
to fall to clouds where
my mother and father sleep
to fall from grace

a graceless leap where
all I need is air
all I need is air to make me fly
to drop me in the sea

all I want is the sea
bipeds on breasts
pulling me like
a submarine or steel-weighted ship
taking me everywhere
pulling me nowhere
all I really want
is to go home

Glory

Walking into my grandmother's kitchen
feels like a slow applause under the skin.

The smell of something two-toned,
baked, or scorched just right
like bramble spices or buttermilk.

On summer Sundays the family Bible
comes out and the tablecloth stays clean.

Bone china, the set reserved for company
little glass jugs of syrup, brown-eyed
Susans picked from their beds, butter

spilling over like a dream, and pears
so green it bows the body inward.

In the corner a dog named Coca sniffs
for scraps or sausage to roll his way.
Don't feed that dog, she says

*I'll be the one cleaning his shitty belly
on the Lord's day, don't feed that dog.*

All is fame for the color burgundy.
Wide-brimmed church hats, heavy tights
cause good girls don't bare naked legs

on Sunday, and her June house dress
that gapped two inches in the front.

Under its folds, the muscles are doughy
from three babies grown, gone.
They all ran to this kitchen, tooth-

gapped, short dark arms stretched
out to say *give me mama, give me.*

When she calls our names now, grand-
daughter one and two, we move
to the table like red ants coming in

from the sun, waiting to nibble biscuits,
holy gossip, and a salty hymn or two.

The First Paradise

There are witnesses to Africa's
big bang   to when earth was water
Restless surface close to the sun
sated phibians   finches   seeds
so many colors all over

Moses drifted by in a cash bucket
his body the shape of a bird
voice speaking haiku
Fish went from water   to air
to skeletal bloom   stone
then   the grapes were planted

Salty rims unbottled the roots
green sugar cane juice followed true
two-headed bison's crowned themselves
kings   and sun-baked stones sizzled
when pissed on

And then song came
sniffing   clawing   pulling at things
pushing through the brown—
pushing through the seven layers
of skin between heart and air whispering
>   *this oven of space*
>   *is where you belong*

To Speak About What Isn't Spoken

The villains should keep you busy.
Jackals and thieves. Holy relics. Stones
of Jordan. Textures of full-bodied nec-
tarines. Mating rites of turtles, or that morning
light which stomps in offering Zen
        secrets and celestial songs.

Did you ever stand guard over
the gate of Thebes? See spears
carved in the backsides of others?
The sharp angles of limbs were bare
yet covered like a pillow in its
        white casing.

Something is growing in my belly.
In dreams I'm alone in a chapel
counting down the days. The tapestries
are draped in smiles. Candles are unlit.
The air is a pew-shaped box and you
        grant wishes.

Something is singing in her bones
and has settled. In dreams her arms
are scarless and smooth. Her brocaded
dress filled with silken plumes, petals,
and the scent of plums. Calcified bones
blaze bright and warm and you
        grant wishes.

There are planes flying over Beirut.
Steel-dipped wings create wounds
in the sky. Rudders and shrapnel
clamor in the gloom, drowning out
the low pulse of valve machines
        beeping in this room.

Can some things stand? Can some things
change? Or will you banish her, like your
other pets—the mammoth, the bison, and
        the dinosaur?

King of the Natural World

Who knows but that on the lower
    frequencies the patterns in the grain,

the right break of a herring bone,
    or the age of root and worm

spoon-fed into tree skin. Grandpa knows
    how to build southern porches

tall enough to see trouble coming;
    the way the palm curves to the right

for the perfect bird call, hammer,
    or alder wood that glints like threads;

how to roast bumblebee husks in April,
    stew crocodile underbelly with land cress

so it seeps from the mouth like sap. He knows
    the first taste of grief rattles the teeth,

like a deep hum into clearings, then slams
    an old body until the belly is full.

I Saw You on the Delta Queen

for Cousin Michael, 2008

The hills of Biloxi have trapped
your voice, warm molasses
bursting in air. I saw you on
the Delta Queen streaming down
river, your skin a battered peach
with eyelashes like fans.
I forget you are dead now.
The coarse sugar of memories
strangled into knots soaked
through like sand. In mirrors a silver
shadow settles over line and limb,
like a hot bruise or two conch
shells pressed together.
Around me I hear an elegy in veils—
island roots pushing through
frogs bleating at shallow ends
and the rattle of brown things at night,
a reminder that I too was once part
of the green and the dirt.
Trudging through fields of old
grape arbors, now I see the dark
bodies of three giant unfurling
avocado trees and it's you—watching
over us like African gods.

Hunger

as a child i would swallow
pits of plums wanting to grow
a garden inside. have stems sprout
from elbows knees like an extra rib
or plump kidney, then i'd move on
to ripe cantaloupes—devour the rind
for its skin cause veins need
flesh to hold onto. if i was
a whale species, i could store food
for days—feed a whole block maybe,
even the exotic fruits. i'd spit out perfectly
formed muscadine grapes. they'd hang
from my mouth like tonsils. i'd have
to be real careful not to break the skin
when i breathe though, real careful.

What We Push Against

At the fruit stand we press
our fingers into the red dimple
of teardrop tomatoes
trying to find what
was offered to the ground
the way Aztecs built *chinampas*—
man-made gardens
from swamp and rinds. How
sweet the first bud
must've tasted—so strong
it made even God jealous.
Like tendering a baby's scalp
we search for the soft spot,
the malleable brain that gives
way to our tips. All the power
rests in the hands: if you
squeeze deep enough
you can feel every ion, every pulse
of the sun. We all start our training
here—learning how to prepare our
dark spots for hiding and living.

The Reaper in Me

Think of the way doctors unpack a body.
Primary colors and cold metal joined just right.

This is not the scar I show—my love
for surgery porn at 1 am, orthopedic
serpents that re-break bones and muscle
memory. Heaven is the sound of tiny mallets,
metacarpals piling on top of each other

like those Haitian boys who fell
through the cracks of the earth—
so fast that even gravity was surprised.
Tiny galaxies formed in their mouths,
a gathering of tongues, souls, and rubble.
Dirt that said *I eat you to live.*

I question those souls and scavengers.
Do you shake the scent of death
from the skull like a woman's shawl,
or does it rest in the crease of hands
and that space between sock and ankle?

I want to be that animal that roots
the ground for peaches, bones, and stars.

The Secret of Living in This Body

Imperfection Begins Early

Take somebody like me
I wasn't born gentle you know

a doctor's blade pulled me out
        feet first
taught me to taste pain
early through twisted limbs

like a jellyfish with bones
        leg braces
were my second skin

made me walk
like a shrunken old woman
at twelve months old

those silver stilts were the brightest
stars in constellation Gemini
        or the rings
of a Jupiter bedspread in August

I was a lesson in geometry
how strong metal is
        the weight
of a child singing *down down baby*

down by the rollercoaster
they all loosened their grips
closed opened eyes
        afraid to see   afraid to touch

my scarred knees and
ironworker feet

Letter to 1991

You're 13 now and Dad still calls you Cimbo,
a nickname we crave to shake loose like
pimples and oatmeal creme Little Debbie
cakes. You worry too much. You worry about
Mom and Dad—the music of something
breaking. It's red with light, all the noise
sometimes. Put your head in a book of sand;
bring your little brother in the back room,
and close the door. There is a suitcase full
of hurt there. And no, you can't unpack it.
Think of that summer when you were six
and your foot slipped into a house of red ants.
The biting up your right leg—the stings
and the buzzing. Mama told you to play
dead like a possum, as rivulets
of alcohol dripped down dark as blood.
The insects fell one by one—dead little bodies
all over the place. Mama held you next
to the fullness of her thighs. You didn't cry.
No hollering or heaving—take hold of that
memory now; rub it between your fingers.
The secret of living in this body is time,
and all the worrying is like walking backwards
on a track. You think I don't know you?
Your favorite word is *Appalachian*
because of the way consonants and vowels
curl around the tongue. This is the time
when you should only dream dreams.
By now you should know that sometimes
you have to write, in order to figure out
what you can never say.

The Human Condition

I shot a gun once
on a dare, and all my fragile parts
shimmied like a two-step
under the skin. The sound clanged
against my ribs, plundered the roots
blocked out everything—
like that night in Georgetown
when I buried my father's mother
and a cold twist seeped
into marrow and spine. I dreamed
of feet moving to a moon dance,
the hearty buffalo with its young
and a white hearse heading
south. Since then I try always to be
a good mammal and resist the current—
the chapped edges of dark
waters, but pennies turn green.
Sometimes I have a fragile mental
skeleton. The wind pushes too far north
like an engine trail or ghost
untamed. If I was a dark root
planted on your windowsill—my stems
would rattle through the night
wanting to taste something bloody
or metallic at the seams.

The Future of Skin

In every dream I wear
a different armor.
In one I'm a wolf
and no one sees
me coming. I keep the wild-
ness at bay,
pick gristle from my teeth—
knowing I've split adverbs
and femurs like Shea butter.

In another I'm a rooster
with silver claws.
I have premonitions
of eclipses and salt-
crusted waters
pulling me
like tiny charges
to new tribes.
Nothing burns, screams,
or crows in alarm.

Or I'm a simple skeleton
free from skin's grip.
Ears small indents and
eye sockets like a painter's
coal with a riot inside.
I step out in the sun
and see skeletons everywhere.
Purses tucked
under bone-shawl blades.
My feet are bare too,
just metatarsals and toe rings

but it's so warm with
skin nowhere to be found
crosses nowhere to be found
the noose nowhere to be found.

House of Magic Rocks

He calls the faded
        picture *Magrita*
or the girl in the red
        dress. She hangs
low on his shopping cart
        to protect his house
of magic rocks—
        grey pea coats that
musk in June
        rusted gold
baby spoons
        cursive on the handle
small dull pieces
        of copper to rub
a collection of yellow
        baseball cards,
with their smell
        he's a boy again
sneaking tobacco
        out of grandmas red tin,
his ashy-kneed brothers
        are colts
shouting about
        Minnie the Moocher
and sweetened apples,
        sugared curls
tugged between them
        like grass.

Dear Black Dress

don't speak to me
don't speak to me about
the hot haze
        that keeps you
        up past midnight

the groove held tight
in your double-stitched
        inseam   it conjures men
like blooming jasmine
        its scent swells
        the mouth

the triangle cinch two quarters down
        pit stop
        to silhouette
shines a light on legs   a well-lit
street to a body
        of currents

i'm not immune to your sorcery
   the sweet feed
        of darkness
the way damp air travels
        from cotton to skin
from skin to mind

you wanna dance—
        with all the shadows
        that bones make
swallow octaves
        cut through   corseted lungs
hips

i try to calm you
       sedate you with pink   cardigans
       beige brown shawls
but it's like covering some hump
   mama deity
      on the prowl
      no marrow is safe

Pitkin Avenue and Stone

I found myself in that store again for the second time
this month, a place the body remembers like a thrash
in the hamstring or the Bob Marley songs we sang

when I was seven. The merchandise has changed
from 49-cent herring to barely dressed Malibu Barbies
and lime green lawn chairs. This is where I learned
to speak, to open mouth wide, and curve palms

to say "give me." My mother would buy sweet meats
and matching barrettes for ponytails that sprawled
from my head like little black arms. I remember
sausage links in bright string, lynchpins, and gummed

toffee that stuck just right to tooth and rib. Today I met
a twin heart washed in salt; an older version of my twenty-
two year old self, where time had pressed little craters

hard on the skin. She was in the hardware aisle wearing
white gloves with pearl buttons, and water dripped
from her skirt like small silver scales leaving a trail

due northeast. Questions rose to the roof of my mouth,
but the topsoil was too thick to speak clearly. I wanted
to say something between a whisper and a prayer

about this store, was there rain outside, this stitch in time,
and this burst in the brain. I wanted to excavate my almost
me chest-deep, but words and letters quickly came undone.

We stepped together as if by surprise, a double-exposed photograph or painting of something caged. I grabbed a piece of chalk and black marker to outline the cross of our bodies and to take note of her scars.

How a Poet Carries Weight

I'm trying not to become
one of those disappearing things—
exotic creatures, a body
covered by afghans, or a face
behind an opaque veil.

I stopped reading *Glamour, Cosmo*
and *Photoshop Weekly* cause
those magazines
they can't handle
the pine beneath my bark,
the lushness in curves
the round rolls above the pubis.

How I glitter
from inside and out,
and write odes to ovaries
playing the samba,
sonnets to the urethra
and contrapuntals of the rib.

How each poem jockeys
for position like climbing up
a complex DNA scale
cause I know how to carry weight—

my mama taught me,
to bind the heart to a cave
of scars, manage all 206 bones
in my body, my sister's body
and yours.

When in doubt I look to Gwendolyn,
Phyllis, and Lucille
standing still in my umbra,
the darkest part of my shadow
and know I can survive
any type of burning.

Blue Hallelujahs

I See a Dirt Road Inside Myself

Longer than a country mile
a shadow—
only I and the dead can see.

It passes by those crooked houses
in the Carolinas, the kind made
of silt, spit, and a board or two.

My uncle with his trailer stands
like clay figurines. Church cornmeal,
cans of Spam, scratch-offs clutched
in hand, tying to keep something at bay
but the wind comes—
the kind that whips, carves out his
dark parts 'til nothing is left.

The road forks at the vee of my chest.
On the left I see the crack
of my father's Dogwood, his hand
splintered by bark, eyes blind
from another ache—my mother

threw piss in his face, and later clothes
in a black Hefty bag. Put my ten-
year-old self on the phone
made me say *daddy, come get your shit.*

The path ends behind my knee.
There you'll find bramble thorns
of cotton, my near-white
grandmother screaming like some-
body rocked you dead, and little
scraps of poems I splash after
to understand it all.

Scrape the Brown Bottom

The sink is full of baby trout, speckled
heads that shimmer at their seams,
moving easily as arms and legs.

They reach for slits of lime and bone-
dry celery in my mother's hand.
There must be a dozen waiting

to simmer in yesterday's broth.
At this time of the month, dimes
battle against the mustard jar

like bullets in a jug. We live *fresh*
as earth-eaters, using what is found
half-price, home-grown, or dented.

She stirs like an old hand working
the soil, keeping mind the time.
Her body remembers in fragments

like pieces of torn paper—Dove soap
and pine, spiced rum cake, medium
baskets of sweet rolls over hymns,

number 2 pencils, gas bills, light
bills, raised tones like voices over
water, and bruised desire that leaves

skin behind. She stirs with a throat half-
closed pouring out cans of tomato,
fleshy hearts for the Crock-Pot base,

knowing like my father's mood,
the gumbo will last three days 'til
its drippings are swallowed clean.

When I Think of My Father

I live in constant fear of extinction,
that I'll be pulled back to muddy toes
and pear trees. Praised for wide hips
and a silent mouth that wants
to scream, echo, grunt, but can't.

Or that I'll meet a man just like my daddy,
tether my back to his name like a spine
where each cord holds large teats filled with children
and more children like little benign tumors.
And when he slips his hand under my skirt
I'll know he doesn't love me—just the malleable
skin that's spreads north and south,
guided by his un-mutable compass.

When I think of my father I can only see
my mother at her knees, chanting *he's gone
Cyn, he's gone*, pairs of discarded
blue jeans on the floor, my mother
fingering the silver buckles like a totem
to lure him back—
from some other woman's scent.

She silently demands my twelve-year old
self to hold and rock her body
like a pair of marsupials—her rooting
my chest for safety, me exposed to the cold
air of their bedroom. I try to be stone,
brine the carnage in my throat
swallow her overripe voice of muscadines.

Falling into the bodies of baggy pants
boys at corner stores—their pockets
full of candy and cake. What they don't
give me, I steal. What I steal, I eat.
I eat to fill a gangrene hole stuffed with bills,
deeds in my father's name, blocks
of state-issued butter and cheese.

I want to take a blade and cut
the edge of this round red wound.
Have daughters born not ready
to fear, but ready to pick up a spade,
dig a ditch, and knife a man.

Dark Fruit

It's the job of the middle daughter
to learn the rituals of sweet roots
and how some can cure a fever
or leave a man sleep-kneed at will.

To know the perfect way to handle over-
ripe peaches, or stock rutabaga soup
for when unwanted company calls.
In the kitchen when it's just us

mama is wigless. Her hands stain green
as she tosses husks of overripe peas
and corn, their curlings spit out like
leavings of a low-paid dock worker.
Like a little brown otter I follow

her movements, holding close those words
in need of shielding—how to reorder
the world through salt, pickle mangoes
set to cure, how to wash underwear

with vinegar and liquid Dawn, keep
a drunk man at bay, or the proper way
to bless the throat on catfish Fridays
to avoid bones. Her lessons always finish

at the market as she claims my limbs
as her own, *press the plum against your
cheek, is the scent fading? it should rest
in the lungs.* Or when tables have spoiled

fruit or sweet potatoes unwashed, *you see
this? this is the way most brown bodies
are used, so keep your legs closed girl.*
I swallow her words like baptismal water.

Passing

: to bind the center of a peach pit heart
like a covered form; to smile tooth-wide
without looking *too* much alive; to cinch
a curved body like a rag; to avoid water-
melon and chicken; to seed thoughts of
bloodline fantasy—*are you one part Indian
or two parts Creole?*; to wear coffee-colored
dresses and cotton headscarves only in the dark;
to unremember the village of old women
who lifted their skirts and birthed you;
to resist the *hush* of spirituals; to enunciate
the *h* and roll your *r's*; to avoid okra and
the black geodes of jazz; to fill the cracks with
dreams of southern porches and plums big
as a well; to pull out the tar-brushed womb;
to drink sweet tea in dainty cups, deliberate
as a geisha waiting to wear new bones again

The Museum

People come here to be dazzled.
To be swept into carefully labeled
history of high yellow and dark skin,
like the slow roll of hands steeped
in trumpets, ivory keys or the bramble
thorns of cotton. Loud speakers trail
all visitors—*did you know this one
invented peanut butter? part of the
light bulb? oh and that lotion
that makes those old kinky strands
cut straight from the root.*

Some exhibits are more popular
than others. Novelty items like
Aunt Jemima's headscarf, yellowed
slave bills of sale, basketball jerseys,
mammy saltshakers, and Obama
bobbleheads are high volume areas.
On the second floor timed to lights
and a smoke machine, a trio of
animatronic colored girls sing
doo doo doo, doodododoo, with plastic
mulatto skin covering their nuts and
bolts. Bobbed hairstyles and silk
chiffon completes the Motown
look, but somehow they seem
solemn in the lights.

Then there's me—*here she is,
here is our last little darkie.
You see the pigmentation here?
We don't let them get that dark*

these days. If pain had a shape
it would be one giant muscle,
it would be the sound the human
mind makes when you realize
you don't own a body anymore.
I've been here for years now.
I can't remember the last time
I saw the sun or felt a taproot
next to my feet, or being in love,
picking juniper berries so thick
they stain my nails like blood coming
clean. I often ask what God wants
from my face and empty body.

When the crowds and tour groups
disperse, my bones ache to
slide side by side in the dark.
Like the bison, dinosaurs, and our
blood brothers the Indians, you'll find
my carcass in this museum—
strings around my pelvis, thin
clear wires making my fluted bones
dance, say hi, in the last great
African mammal display.

Blue Hallelujahs from the Hand

after Carrie Mae Weems' Kitchen Table Series

In the right light I'm beautiful.

Covered in flour and paprika
balled cubes of meat,
you can still see patterns
fault lines in the palm center;

the first throw of jacks
and rocks when I was six,
golden frogs that bleed
and bleep so high;

a body twirl in Sunday's best
colored swan lake
smoothed gloves in church peach;

the steam of the hot comb
the weight of it
cause nappy heads can't hold
cherry barrettes or the sound
of light-skinned caramel boys;

grandmother's words—
*you have to pull flesh
from the throat not the belly,
you are two kins away*

*from pulled cotton,
don't waste any part of the pig
stir hog soup when cold comes;*

the cool wash of river
on stiff limbs when death came, settled
her like a nesting doll;

all was changed with corn whiskey
out of fruit jars, and fingers
trailing the land of bodies
twice licked;

Christ is amazed
with taffy babies
those shriveled sweet things—
with vein-rich palms of their own.

In the kitchen I'm beautiful.

Garlic and onion shines brown
in the light, and fistfuls of mackerel
cover nails at the seams—

it tempers a woman
cause the muscle knows
how to wield a knife
and hold close salted migrations.

Acknowledgments

Versions of these poems have appeared in the following publications:

African American Review: "The Museum" and "What I Know About Blues"
BLACKBERRY: a magazine: "Blue Hallelujahs from the Hand," "The First Paradise," and "Inside the Rolling Walls: A Fairytale"
Box of Jars: "Letter to 1991"
Callaloo: "Revolution Staccato in B"
The Cossack Review: "To Speak About What Isn't Spoken"
The Dead Mule School of Southern Literature: "Ethel September"
DMQ Review: "House of Magic Rocks"
Fjords Review: Black American Edition: "When I Think of My Father"
Gemini Magazine: "I Saw You on the Delta Queen"
HEArt: Human Equity Through Art: "How a Poet Carries Weight" and "Mind the Gap"
Kweli Journal: "What Lies Beneath," "The Sun Don't Know," and "King of the Natural World"
Kinfolks: a journal of black expression: "The Shop Washington Built"
Muzzle Magazine: "Passing"
Obsidian: Literature in the African Diaspora: "Venue Change"
Passages North: "The Reaper in Me"
PoetryMagazine.com: "Things I Carry Into the World"
Poetry City, USA: "2 am"
Saint Ann's Review: "What We Push Against"
Sou'wester: "Dear Black Dress"
Spillway Magazine: "Imperfection Begins Early" and "Let Me Dance While I Dream"
Tidal Basin Review: "Recipe for Consummation," "Scrape the Brown Bottom," "The Hip Collective," and "The Husband in Contrast"
The Wide Shore: A Journal of Global Women's Poetry: "Glory"

My deepest gratitude to the editors of journals where my poems have appeared; thank you for opening up a space for me. Thank you Cave Canem Foundation and the Callaloo Creative Writing Workshop, you are a bouquet of black roses I take with me always; Leigh Stein and the Brooklyn Poets family; mentors Nikky Finney, Tyehimba Jess, Vievee Francis, Linda Susan Jackson, Hettie Jones, and Lyrae Van Clief-Stefanon; poet compatriots Lolita Stewart-White, Pamela Taylor, Nikia Chaney, and Safia Jama; poets-in-arms Amber Atiya, Ed Toney, and JP Howard; and poet ancestors Lucille Clifton and Gwendolyn Brooks for creating a brick road for us to follow. To my ancestral kin who whisper in my ear, thank you. To my family, you know who you are, thank you for your unending support and encouragement.

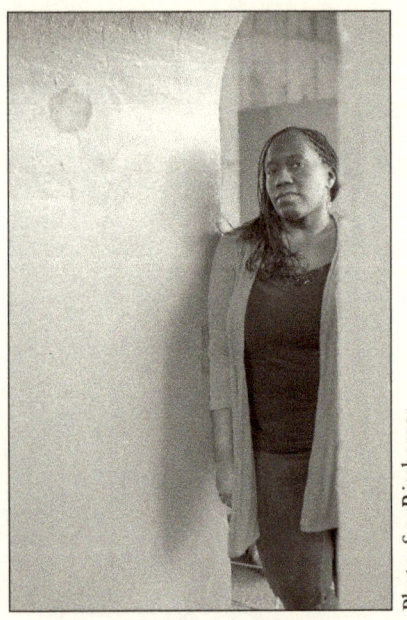

Photo: Sue Rissberger

Cynthia Manick is a Pushcart Prize nominated poet with a MFA in Creative Writing from the New School; she has received fellowships from Cave Canem, the Callaloo Creative Writing Workshop, Fine Arts Work Center, the Hambidge Center for the Creative Arts & Sciences, Hedgebrook, Poets House, and the Vermont Studio Center. She was a 2014 finalist for the New York Foundation of Arts Fellowship in Poetry; serves as East Coast Editor of the independent press Jamii Publishing; and is Founder of the reading series Soul Sister Revue. Manick's work has appeared in *African American Review, Bone Bouquet, Callaloo, Fjords Review, Kweli Journal, Muzzle Magazine, Obsidian: Literature in the African Diaspora, St. Ann's Review, Spillway Magazine,* and elsewhere. She currently resides in Brooklyn, New York.